Hard Time in the County Jail
One Officer's Experience

Rita Roark

PublishAmerica
Baltimore

© 2006 by Rita Roark.
All rights reserved. No part of this book may be reproduced, stored in a retrieval system or transmitted in any form or by any means without the prior written permission of the publishers, except by a reviewer who may quote brief passages in a review to be printed in a newspaper, magazine or journal.

First printing

At the specific preference of the author, PublishAmerica allowed this work to remain exactly as the author intended, verbatim, without editorial input.

ISBN: 1-4241-3728-4
PUBLISHED BY PUBLISHAMERICA, LLLP
www.publishamerica.com
Baltimore

Printed in the United States of America

Dedication

I dedicate this book to my one and only son, Lonnie Prachyl; his loving wife, Cindy; my endearing grandchildren, Keenan, Valery, and Stevie; and to my wonderful and supportive husband, Kit.

Acknowledgments

To my daughter-in-law, Cindy: Her assistance was truly appreciated. I thank my friend Pat Pratt for her expert help in editing this manuscript. Finally, I thank my friend Mare Stanton for all her helpful suggestions and computer experience.

Protect thy dignity
As thine own heart,
Surely, thy spirit
Shall survive.

Rita Roark

1

At age forty-five, I wanted to do something about the drab, ordinary existence my life had become. I decided to change jobs and do something a little less predictable, so I went to work in the county jail.

On my very first day I realized I had entered a whole new world, a world of inmates yelling, sliders clanging, and continuous radio traffic. The officers on their radios were speaking a language I did not understand. I knew I had strayed far from predictable. A female officer escorted me through the jail. I was a little frightened, but was determined not to let the inmates know.

As we walked through one area, the male inmates began yelling at us. One threw his whole body against the tank Plexiglas window. I looked back expecting to see the glass in pieces on the cement floor.

From there we entered the Maximum Security area. One of the male inmates stared at me intently. A chill ran down my spine. I felt he was looking right through me with the coldest blue eyes I had ever seen. I felt like an unsavory piece of meat that would eventually be eaten, anyway.

I looked away as if I hadn't noticed him as the slider closed behind me. The female officer asked if I was okay. I answered "yes," but it was all I could do to keep my legs from running out of there.

She was called to the captain's office and asked me to wait in the break room until she returned. As I entered the break room, I noticed a large black man making fresh coffee. He didn't seem to notice my entrance, and I had an opportunity to watch him for a moment. He seemed very relaxed, as though he was at home in his own kitchen. As he turned around, he saw me standing there and greeted me with a big smile.

"Hello," he said. "Can I offer you a great cup of coffee?"

I had already enjoyed two cups that morning and knew one more might have me bouncing off the wall.

"No, thank you," I said, politely.

He told me he was the floor trustee and he was there to help the officers.

A little boldly I asked him why he was incarcerated. He told me that he wasn't really a criminal; he was there on tax evasion charges. I felt a little more at ease, knowing I was not in the company of a rapist or murderer.

My guide returned and introduced me as a new officer to the floor trustee.

"Good luck," he said, and smiled again.

As we walked down the hallway, I told her the floor trustee had admitted that he was incarcerated on tax evasion charges and that he had treated me respectfully while I had waited for her to return.

She laughed. "Well, I guess you could call it tax evasion. I doubt that he paid taxes on the money he made from the drugs he was selling."

I laughed at myself for being so gullible. I had a lot to learn if I was going to survive in this place. Perhaps that was why the trustee was smiling as I walked away.

2

My second day on the job I began to find out what it's really like being an officer in an understaffed facility. The sergeant took me to the pod in the female area and showed me how to open the tank doors using a lighted electric panel that was laid out like a blueprint with all the cell numbers on it. The pod is an approximately 6 x 6 enclosed area where the officer sits with windows facing the tank so the prisoners can be seen. She handed me the food pass key while vaguely explaining how to use it.

"I'll be back later to check on you," she said. "If you have any problems, call me on the radio."

"Call me on the radio," I thought. I'm not sure I know how to operate the radio and even if I did, what would I say?"

"Help!"

As she was leaving, she turned back and said, "By the way, do not give any of the females toilet paper unless they turn in an empty roll. They've been stuffing rolls in the air vents. They think it's too cold down here."

As soon as she left the area, the females began to demand the toilet paper, but refused to give me an empty roll. For two hours, until my sergeant returned, I went through the hell of being initiated into the system. The inmates did their best to make my life miserable. They were relentless, but so was I. I did not give them any toilet paper.

When I look back on that situation, the whole ordeal seems childish; a way for the prisoners to get attention and "try the rookie." I was following orders. The inmates hoped I hadn't been informed of procedure, but when they realized I had, used whatever bullying tactics they could to wear me down. I wonder, now, if it was worth the effort. I could have quieted the disturbances by giving into their demands but I had my orders. If they had remained fully dressed, they wouldn't have been cold.

3

When I first started to work in the jail there was no training program for officers. Everyone was thrown into the job and, hopefully, could survive. The inmates were allowed to yell, dance on the day room tables, run out into the hallway when the tank doors were opened, and even curse the officers. Nothing was done about the riotous situation. The female inmates would lay their heads on the floor beside the tank doors and scream across the hallway to the male inmates. When they weren't screaming back and forth, they were sliding notes under the door.

Officers are not supposed to pass anything for an inmate nor allow them to pass anything to each other. However, as in all walks of life, this sometimes happened.

The inmates were always trying to get the officers involved with them in some way, hoping to get a little something extra; all hoping the officer would bring them extra food, magazines, or cigarettes from the outside. Some officers provided small favors to the inmates. Various inmates even asked for officers' addresses, on the pretext of keeping in touch. One of the most difficult things to do is to try to keep that line drawn between the officer and the inmate.

Several months after I began the job, a training program was developed for the officers, which really helped. We had a set of rules to follow and so did the inmates. Now we could write disciplinary reports when inmates did not follow the rules of the jail. This helped to control the inmates to a point. I was one of the first officers to follow through with the "disciplinaries." Once the inmates realized that the officer would take the time to write the disciplinary and they would suffer the consequences, the situation became a little easier to control.

A floor trustee works on each floor of the facility, and when I first began working in the jail, I considered the trustee a fellow employee, even though I knew he was an inmate. The floor trustee's job is to help the officers by getting the cleaning supplies together and keeping the jail clean. He also brings coffee to the officers if asked. Because he works out on the floor, you tend to view him differently. Most were in jail on lesser crimes and sometimes they would discuss their personal situations with the officers. Women were not used as trustees because of the sexual undercurrent.

The trustee on our floor when I first started working in the jail was very likable and helpful. When he brought the cleaning supplies for the inmates to use, the officer for that area would open the tank doors so the supplies could be left. There were times when the officer was not in the area where the supplies needed to go and the trustee would ask me to open the tank doors for him. I didn't mind because I knew he had a job to do and didn't want him to have to wait for the officer in charge to let him pass.

When I reported for work one day, I found our floor trustee lying on the floor handcuffed and shackled. He was screaming and cursing my sergeant. Unknown to me, he had gotten drugs into the jail and was passing them to the other inmates in the mop buckets.

That was my first lesson. Don't trust the trustees, they have their own agenda! I learned to do what I could for myself. Counting on the trustee too much means being expected to look the other way when he is following his agenda. There have been times it would have been easier to look the other way when an inmate was not following the rules of the jail, but doing that would give him reason to go one step further the next time, and one day I would arrive for work and find another floor trustee handcuffed and shackled on the floor.

4

Each day when an officer reports for duty, he or she is assigned an area of work for that shift. The first and most important objective is to walk through the area and get a head count. The second is to make sure the inmates are following the rules of the jail.

In most jails, an officer is not allowed to enter a Maximum Security area without another officer being present. Because we were shorthanded most of the time, that wasn't always possible at county jail.

One day as I was walking alone through the Maximum Security area gathering my head count, I heard the tank door suddenly slam closed. I called for an officer to come to my pod and open the tank door, but no one responded. I looked down from the upstairs walkway as the male inmates watched me, assuming that I would panic. The thought suddenly occurred to me that I was surrounded by accused murderers, rapists, and thieves. I realized this could become a real problem for a female officer without backup, but I didn't want the inmates to know I was afraid, so I continued on with my head count.

After finishing the head count, I walked down the stairs and over to the tank door. I called again on my radio, but still there was no answer. Each cell has an intercom for the inmates to use in case of an emergency. One of the inmates used his to call the Central Control, and finally an officer arrived to open the door. I assumed one of the inmates had closed the door on purpose to scare me, but found out later that another officer had closed the door thinking it had accidentally been left open.

Another time while working the same area, I was walking through and doing my head count around 7 a.m. when I noticed a couple of inmates in the Day Room in their boxers. The Day Room is a large room with iron tables, benches, and a television. Most inmates consider it their living room. It is a jail rule that all inmates must be dressed while in the Day Room. I asked both inmates to get their clothes on while I continued with my head count. One of the inmates went back into his cell, but the other stood obstinately in the Day Room in his underwear. I asked him again to get dressed and then I left the tank to resume my duties.

I entered the pod where I could look through the Plexiglas window into the Day Room. There he stood glaring back at me. I tapped on the window and told him again to put on some clothes. Suddenly, he ran over to the window and hit it full force with his fist. Startled, I jumped back. Fortunately, the glass held up against his vicious blow. My face would surely not have fared as well if he'd hit me. He then began to scream at me, "I hate you and everybody in this mother fucking jail!"

I was so upset about his tirade I lost my temper and opened the tank door, walked over and I looked up at him. He was head and shoulders taller and outweighed me by at least 150 pounds, but I was so angry that it didn't matter at the time.

I advised him I did not care that he hated me and everybody in the jail, and I did not make up the rules. I also reminded him he had received a copy of the rules when he was booked in, and those rules applied to everyone. I told him again to put his clothes on or he would be locked in his cell for the rest of the day. I slammed the tank door loudly as I left. My sergeant heard all the commotion and hurried down to my area. I explained the situation and he ordered the inmate to get dressed, which he did.

I said to myself, "I really believe that I would like to start my morning off a little differently." Unfortunately, bad days come around often in county jail.

We had one inmate who would constantly throw temper tantrums to get attention. One afternoon, he sent in three med requests on separate sheets, even though the inmates had been told that all med requests were to be written on one sheet. I was assisting the nurse with the med requests when the officer brought me the inmate's three requests. I asked the officer to remind the inmate to use one request sheet. When informed of the rules, the inmate began screaming and kicking the tank door. The officer working that area was a new recruit and I wasn't sure he could handle the inmate by himself. I walked over to assist him, and tried to explain to the inmate about using one request, but he was in a rage and hit the Plexiglas window with his fist and kicked the tank door again. He screamed at me, "I'll kill you, I'll kill you, bitch!" and demanded that the other officer open the door so he could get to me.

Normally, when a situation like this arises, an officer, for his or her own safety, calls for backup. I was having a very stressful day before this situation occurred, and didn't react with customary caution.

To get his attention, I hit the window the same way he had. This action really made him angry—someone was mimicking his act. He continued to demand that the door be opened so he could get to me.

I got so disgusted with his ranting I decided to call his bluff. I told the other officer to open the tank door, but he refused. I told him again to open the door and if the inmate attacked me, he was to pull him off. I had already decided I would not back off. When the door opened, he came rushing out toward me, but I did not move. When he saw I was not going to step aside, he stepped around me and began to yell at the other officer who had already called for backup. Several officers responded and the inmate was taken to Solitary Confinement to be locked down. The other inmates in the tank had seen this inmate throw these fits many times and were glad someone had finally called him on it. They all began to applaud, and for that one day, I was their hero, a dubious honor at best.

5

If an inmate feels he has been mistreated in some way, he may file a grievance against the officer or the jail facility. The officer is allowed to respond to the Grievance Officer on his own behalf. The grievance is reviewed and a decision made, based on the merits of the grievance. If the officer is deemed to be wrong and the incident bad enough, the officer could lose his or her job. Lesser charges receive a write-up that goes on his or her record. If the inmate is found to be wrong, the incident is usually dismissed. This causes more of a problem for the officer than the inmate, so many grievances are written. The inmate has nothing to lose, but for the officer, a lot is at stake.

In a jail, it is very important the male and female inmates be kept separated. I was working the Maximum Security area and had opened the tank door to pick up the food trays. The officer working the female area was escorting a female back to her area, which was down this same hallway. As I pulled the trays out of the tank, one of the male inmates stepped into the hallway. I asked him to step back because the female was just a few feet away, but he refused to move. I put my hand on his shoulder and asked him again to step back. He became very upset because I touched him but I finally managed to close the tank door.

Later, I discovered he had filed a grievance against me stating that I had propositioned him and touched him inappropriately—in his words, "rubbed all over him." I had turned in an incident report concerning the situation the day it happened, and, luckily, the Disciplinary Board believed my version of the incident.

As stated earlier, the male and female inmates were constantly sliding notes across the hallway to each other, and we were on constant vigil to catch the offenders and confiscate the notes. In one incident, the male inmates were aware I was closely monitoring my hallway because they could hear my radio traffic, which goes on twenty-four hours a day. They became angry because they could not pass their notes. I left my area for a minute and when I returned there was a note lying in the hallway. I picked it up and read it hoping the writer had signed his name. The inmates usually use an alias to keep from being recognized, but this one had signed his last name. It was obvious that the note was written hoping I would find it and be insulted. The words were very rude and hurtful, saying, among other things, I was very ugly and was jealous of the females because I could not get a man. The note also made fun of my hair and called me a man-woman.

I showed the note to an officer working the pod in that area, and as he was reading it, I saw the inmate I thought had written it standing in the Day Room looking at me and smiling. It was obvious he was receiving great pleasure knowing I had read his insults. I checked his handwriting against a request he had signed earlier for verification, and found it to be the same. Another officer and I entered his tank and I advised him he would be locked down for twenty-four hours and a disciplinary written on his actions. He admitted he had written the note, and then yelled, "Lock me down! I don't give a damn! I just got my time—twenty years—that don't bother me. I can do that standing on my dick!"

I told him that hopefully he would get that opportunity. As we locked him in his cell, I encouraged him to have a nice day.

As I left the tank, I had a mental picture of him doing his twenty years in the position he had so rudely stated, but in my mind he was spinning around and around like a top. The mental picture made me smile. I've heard sometimes the best offense is a good defense; well, sometimes it's necessary to defend the mind against the offensive. The offensive can lurk around any corner in the county jail.

6

Every work day was a battle, usually a battle of words only. There were some inmates who followed the rules of the jail and others who did not. Most of the offenders of the rules were male inmates who did not want a woman telling them what to do.

One of the jail rules was that clothing could not be hung on the upstairs railings because it gives a bad appearance. This was a constant problem because the inmates washed their clothing out by hand and hung it on the rails to dry.

The sergeant made periodic walk-throughs of each area, and having clothing hung on the rails reflected on the duty officer's ability to maintain control. The only item that could be placed on the rail was a blanket, and then only while inmates were showering when a female officer was on duty, as there were no shower doors.

One particular inmate, who was incarcerated for murder and had allegedly been hired to kill someone, caused considerable problems. I had argued with him several times about clothing on the rails, but when I entered the tank, I noticed laundry hanging on the rails again and asked the inmates in the tank to remove it.

The accused murderer walked up to me and proceeded to talk over me. Another inmate in the tank joined in, and before long, my voice could no longer be heard. He yelled to the inmates on the upstairs walkway that I told them to pull down the blanket in front of the shower. I knew someone was in the shower because I could see the bottom half of his legs, and I certainly did not tell anyone to remove the blanket. The inmate was attempting to embarrass me in front of everyone in the tank. I began to get upset with this man, and I'm sure the inmate in the shower was not too happy when the blanket was pulled off the railing.

He continued to argue with me and finally I called the corporal who was in charge of the shift when the sergeant was not there. When he arrived, the inmate told him there were no problems in the tank except when I was working that area. The inmate berated me for about ten minutes while my corporal just stood there. The corporal is supposed to back you up when you are trying to enforce the jail rules, but he just stood there and allowed the inmate to rant and rave. The inmate had won the battle. I finally just walked away.

Later, I spoke with my corporal and asked him why he did not defend me. He did not give me any reason, but did say he was sorry. I didn't feel his insincere apology covered the humiliation that I had endured.

Once again, I faced the same problem with the same inmate, but this time I had decided to try a different angle. I approached him about his clothing on the rails and explained to him I did not make the rules of the jail, but it was my job to make sure that the rules were followed. I told him I had a job to do and I had to do it to the best of my ability. I asked him if he were out in the world doing whatever he did for a living, would he not also want to do that job to the best of his abilities? I reminded him again I was only doing my job when I asked him to remove his clothing from the rails. He stood there looking at me with a half grin on his face. He then walked over and pulled the clothing off the rail. I think we finally understood one another.

7

We had an inmate who was arrested for drug trafficking and rumor was that he was connected to the Mexican Mafia. He was housed in the sick tank because he had diabetic seizures. I worked in that area quite often, but did not know him better than any other inmate, although there were times he had a seizure and I was there to help him through it. Perhaps that is why he felt he could trust me.

The inmate had agreed to work with one of the undercover officers after being promised a lighter sentence for his cooperation. The plan was for him to use the phone in the tank to get the information on drug deals.

I was asked by my superiors to call the undercover officer when said inmate had some information he could use. This was a very secretive situation because the inmate was afraid for his life. I would contact the undercover officer and he would have me bring the inmate to a room downstairs where he could talk with him privately. The other inmates in his tank were left with the impression that he left the tank to visit his attorney. This continued for a couple of months.

Later, there was a big drug bust thanks to the information given by this inmate. He did receive a lighter sentence and was finally sent to prison. Before he left, he wrote a letter to me and left it with one of the other inmates to give to me.

In the letter he thanked me for helping him and said his goodbyes. He then listed the address of his sister and asked me to write her. Also, he stated that I could get his new address from her and that he hoped that I would write him. In the letter he referred to me as "His Butterfly." He was acting like we had some kind of love relationship going on.

I was shocked. I was also very upset that he had involved another inmate when he gave him the letter to give to me. I took the letter straight to my captain and told him that I never wanted to be involved as a go-between in any drug deal again.

As time passed, I imagined the inmate wondered why I never contacted his sister and I was very relieved that he never tried to contact me. I felt very anxious about the whole situation for a long time.

8

Often the inmates got into fights and the officers would have to break them up. When an officer hears the backup call on the radio, they try to respond as soon as possible.

One day a fight broke out in the sick tank and I called for backup. For some reason, no one responded except my sergeant. He was a small built man, but he did not let that stop him. He ran into the tank and tried to break up the fight. The two inmates and my sergeant were wrestling on the cement floor. I kept expecting other male officers to arrive, but they did not. I realized I was going to have to get involved. The two inmates and my sergeant were so entwined that you could not tell where one man began and another one ended.

An arm stuck out of the pile reaching toward me. I grabbed the arm and slowly pulled. It was one of the inmates ready to give up the fight. Had he not been ready to quit, I don't know what I'd have done. I was not ready to join the brawl.

My sergeant and I were both relieved when the fight ended. Both inmates were locked down for fifteen days and several of the officers were written up for not listening to their radios, putting two officers at risk.

Sometimes, the inmates would get into fights and the nurse would not be available. When this happened, the officers would have to tend to the wounds or call EMS to take them to the hospital to be examined.

Several inmates in the jail had tested positive for AIDS; therefore, we were always told to wear gloves when confronted with a bloody situation.

One afternoon two inmates got into a fight and one of the inmates was severely injured. He was brought to the Med Room where I was supposed to clean him up and the sergeant would make the decision to send him to the hospital. There was blood all over his swollen face.

As I was attempting to clean his face, a chunk of flesh fell out of his forehead and hit the floor. When I examined his head, there was a hole about one-half inch deep and an inch wide in his forehead. I picked up the piece of flesh and put it in a plastic bag to be taken with him to the hospital. I felt sick to my stomach, but I continued to clean the blood off the inmate, while putting pressure on the wound.

When I first came to work in the jail, I was one of those people who could not stand the sight of blood, but as time passed, I got over it.

9

It is not true that just because a person works in a jail they are threatened or in threatening situations on a daily basis. It is always a possibility, though very seldom does it actually happen. An officer may become involved in a fight while trying to break up a fight between inmates, but rarely does an inmate attack an officer, although they will attack you verbally. This can be handled in different ways. Some officers just take it and walk off while others write a disciplinary on the inmate. If a disciplinary is written, the inmate could lose his or her visitation or commissary privileges.

I had only one fight with a female in the eight years that I worked in the jail. I came very close several times, but backup would arrive in time to end the confrontation.

There was a female throwing a tantrum in the Day Room, which was upsetting to me and the other females in the tank. I knew if the situation continued, there would be a fight in the tank.

As I entered the tank, I told the irate female to go into her house (cell) and close the door. She started up the stairs, but stopped about halfway up. I told her again to go to her cell but she refused and dared me to make her go into her cell.

I called for backup and then started up the stairway. When I reached her, I grabbed her by her arm to lead her to her cell. She pulled away from me and with her hands on my arms she tried to push me down the stairs. The other females in the tank began to yell that she had AIDS and that I should not touch her.

I looked around for backup but no one arrived. I realized I could be fighting for my life. She had the leverage because she was above me and I knew I could easily lose my balance and fall down the stairs. We wrestled for a while and then she slipped past me and ran down the stairs with me following. She ran out the tank door and started down the hallway. I saw my sergeant and captain headed toward her so I yelled for them to stop her. The female sergeant tripped her and she fell to the floor. She was then cuffed and taken to a lockdown cell.

I strained my back in the scuffle and had to go to a chiropractor the next day. I also sprained my thumb, but considering the circumstances, it could have been worse.

Later, I asked several of the officers why they had not responded when I called. They said they had not heard the call. There was so much noise in the female tank it had blocked my call.

I learned yet another lesson that day. Don't get into a confrontation on the stairway and always wait for backup before entering the tank.

The female I had the fight with was sent to a mental hospital and returned to the jail six months later. When she re-entered the jail, I was called to search her, spray her with lice disinfectant, and make sure she showered and dressed in her jail uniform. I was hesitant when I realized who she was, but she was very calm and gave me no problems. Eventually, I asked her if she remembered me. She said she did and apologized for her previous behavior.

10

Another day, I was working the Maximum Security area. As I was walking through to do my head count, this inmate came up to me demanding a request sheet. I advised him as soon as I finished my count, I would get him one. He appeared to be very agitated. He was yelling and disturbing the whole tank. It was approximately 7 a.m. and most of the inmates were still sleeping. Before I could finish my count, he was up in my face yelling again.

He screamed, "I have mental problems and I want to see the captain, now!" I told him that the captain was busy and that he could fill out a request and ask to speak to him. I then gave him three requests. He told me that he did not trust me to take the request to the captain. I advised him that he could give his request to the next officer that passed by.

Because he kept screaming, he woke up the other inmates in the tank and one of them shouted to him, "Shut the hell up!" That did not set well with him and it became obvious that the two were going to get into a fight.

I called for backup and when they arrived, he told the sergeant he needed a request and I had refused to give him one. After talking with the sergeant for a while, he finally agreed to go into his cell and his door was then locked.

We did not have an empty cell downstairs, so he was left in the tank. Some of the cell door locks were damaged and if kicked repeatedly, they could come open. I reminded my sergeant about the cell doors in that tank, but I was told that the inmate could not be moved. At least he had calmed down and there was peace and quiet in the tank.

After about five minutes, the screaming and kicking of the door began. He was calling me filthy names and once again the whole tank was disturbed. Before long, my nerves were shot. I advised my sergeant concerning the situation but nothing was done.

I had brought a Dr. Pepper to drink on my break and realizing that I could not leave my pod, I decided to drink it and pretend I was having a pleasant day. As I opened my Dr. Pepper, it began to spew out the top of the bottle all over my desk, my uniform, and then ran down my arm and dripped off my elbow. I started to clean up the mess when suddenly I realized that the noise from the inmate had stopped. The quiet made me very uneasy. I glanced over to his cell door and there he was. He had kicked open his cell door and was standing there stark naked. His teeth were clenched as he screamed, "Kill me bitch, kill me!" I decided not to concern myself with cleaning up my Dr. Pepper.

I called for backup. When they arrived and saw the situation, a Solitary Confinement cell was emptied and he was moved downstairs immediately. He would not put on his clothes, so he was restrained and escorted down the elevator completely naked. I could still hear him screaming as I headed back to my pod to drink what was left of my Dr. Pepper and finish my day.

11

One night I was walking down the Maximum Security hallway with a couple of officers when I heard a banging noise coming from the Maximum Security area. I opened the pod door and looked around to see what was going on. When I looked to my left, I saw an inmate hanging from the second floor railing with his county sheets tied around his neck. I called for backup, opened the tank door, and ran in.

A couple of officers responded, but the sergeant had not yet arrived.

His face was purple in color and his body was limp. He was hanging halfway between the first and second floor.

We were not allowed to have scissors in our pods. The only scissors we had were downstairs. By the time someone could get down the elevator, grab the scissors, and get back up the elevator, the inmate would surely be dead.

I stood under the inmate and tried to push him upward as to relieve some of the pressure on his neck, but that did not seem to help the situation. I felt something wet dripping from the inmate and down my arms. It was urine.

Some of the other inmates were up on the second floor trying to untie the knots in the sheet so he could be lowered to the floor.

They were all frantic and doing the best they could to try to save him. Two officers were also trying to untie the sheets.

When I realized that the knots could not be untied fast enough to save him, I told the officers and the inmates to pull him up slowly. They screamed at me, "If we pull him up, he could break his neck!"

I yelled back, "If you don't pull him up so we can get that sheet off his neck, he will die anyway!" They pulled him up very slowly while he dangled lifelessly. Finally, he was lying on the upstairs walkway.

The sergeant arrived and together with a couple of other officers, they untied the knots. Another of the officers performed CPR.

The color began to return to the inmate's face and he opened his eyes. He tried to talk, but could not be understood as his voice was raspy. He was coughing and shaking uncontrollably.

EMS arrived and transported the inmate to the hospital. After being examined, it was determined he was going to be okay. His neck had not been broken and he had no brain damage from the lack of oxygen. We were all amazed.

For several months after that I had flashbacks. Whenever I would enter that pod, I would look over to my left and for a split second, I would see him hanging there. I will *never* forget it.

12

As I mentioned before, the officers get to know the trustees better than the other inmates mainly because they are out on the floor every day. They were not allowed to give anything to the officers or take anything from them.

One trustee was in jail because he had written hot checks to get money for his drug addiction. He had also stolen blank prescriptions from his father, who was a doctor. He was a good trustee and basically a good person.

In our jail, the inmates were not allowed to have radios because they pulled the wires out of them to make tattoo guns.

Our floor trustee was talking to me one day about how he missed his music. He enjoyed jazz music and before he was incarcerated, he and his friends would hang out all night in a downtown jazz club. He was a real music lover.

I love music myself, but not necessarily jazz. He had mentioned a jazz musician that he favored. I decided maybe it was time for me to buy a jazz tape. Although I could not give him the tape, I had a tape player and I could play it loud enough for him to hear it as he walked down the hallway. I frequented several stores before finding the music he enjoyed.

When I arrived at work, I was asked to help the nurse with her filing. I put the tape in and waited for the music to lead him in my direction. He walked up to the door where I was filing and just stood there. I will never forget the look on his face. He was smiling from ear to ear and I almost thought I saw tears in his eyes.

He asked me if I had bought the tape for him. I lied and told him I had not. For the next month we listened to jazz music every day while I was at work. He became a much happier person and his time served in our jail became a little easier.

I remember thinking that it doesn't take much of an effort to make someone happy, and thanks to him, I learned to enjoy jazz music, too.

Later, he was sent to prison. One day, I was working the Central Control area when the phone rang. He called me by my name. At first, I did not recognize his voice, but when he mentioned the jazz singer's name, I knew. He told me that he was out and was doing okay. I asked him if he had stayed out of trouble while he was in prison and he stated that he had. He also told me that he had gotten a job and was working in Dallas, Texas. I told him that I was proud of him and encouraged him to have a good life.

"You were not forgotten," he said. "You made a difference in my life when I needed it most and I just wanted to thank you for that." We said our goodbyes and I never heard from him again.

13

There was one incident that affected me more than any other. We had an inmate who was kept isolated near the book-in area. He was separated from the other inmates because he was in the latter stages of AIDS.

He was in his early twenties, medium build, with light brown hair and blue eyes. His skin was so pale that it seemed almost transparent. Whenever the nurse was not available, it was my duty to take his medication to him.

In the beginning, he walked over to the food pass to take his medication, but as time passed he was too weak, so I had to enter his cell to hand him his medication. Sometimes when I handed him his pills, he shook so hard that the pills flew across his bunk, and I had to help him find them. I gave him some water to take the meds with and he would spill it everywhere. He tried to stand up but his legs would not cooperate. It was as though his brain could not register what was happening to his body. Finally, toward the end, I had to drop the pills in his mouth and hold the cup of water above his face and let it run into his mouth.

A couple of days later, I took his vitals and found his blood pressure to be very low. As I leaned over him, I realized that his sheets were soaking wet and after further inspection, I found that his clothes were also wet all the way down to his socks. I have no idea how long he had been lying in his own urine.

The nurse had left a package of adult diapers in the book-in area the week before and I heard her tell the book-in officer to give them to the inmate, as he needed them.

As I entered the book-in area, I saw the diapers lying on the floor unopened.

I asked the officer why she had not been giving him the diapers and she stated, "It is not my job to take care of these AIDS inmates and I am not going to do it." I asked her if she realized that the inmate was lying in urine. She said that she didn't realize because she had been very busy and had not checked on him and then added that she did not care.

I called the nurse and advised her concerning the situation. I told her his blood pressure was very low and I felt that he should be taken to the hospital because I was afraid he was going to die. I reminded her that his clothing was wet with urine and asked her if I could get him into something dry. She told me to wear double gloves and to be very careful. One of the other female officers was studying to be a nurse, so I called her to come and assist me.

As I entered his cell, he looked at me as though I was an angel sent from heaven. He began speaking words I could not understand. We stripped off the sheets and then covered him with a blanket while we removed his clothing. The smell of urine was stifling. Finally, we managed to replace his wet clothing.

The other officer left and I waited with him until the ambulance arrived to transport him to the hospital.

His pale blue eyes were locked on mine and a weak smile was on his face. I wondered if maybe he thought I was his mother. The ambulance arrived and took him away. I never saw him again.

Somehow, I had managed to keep myself together during the whole ordeal. I entered the elevator to go back upstairs, but as soon as the door closed I began to cry uncontrollably. Where is his family? Don't they care? Do they even know where he is?

I thought about my own son.

Later, I asked if he had ever had any visitors and was told that no one had ever come to see him. A few days later, I was told he had died. I cried again. He had died without any family or friends to comfort him and spent his last days lying in urine in a jail cell. This was one of the saddest moments I had ever experienced.

I thought of him daily for a long time. I decided that I wanted to do something in his memory. I wrote this poem:

As he lay there trembling, I approached his bed.
A flattened mattress supported his head.
His eyes were hollow, his body frail.
The scent of urine, an unwanted smell.

He tried to stand, but hit the floor.
I stood there staring through his cell door.
I unlocked the door and took his hand.
The face of innocence, this childish man.

No family or friends to lessen his cry.
A moment between strangers, a soulful sigh.
I washed his body and covered him well.
With torn cotton sheets from the county jail.

As I turned to leave, he tried to speak.
But a frigid smile was his retreat.
He left that day, no need for goodbyes.
I will never forget the look in his eyes.

14

I had been working in the jail approximately six months when I had an anxiety attack. Continuous stress affects a person in many different ways.

After working the same area for a long period of time, the inmates really tend to get on your nerves. I had worked the female area for three weeks straight without being rotated to another area. Most female officers found it easier to work the areas with male inmates because the female inmates are more argumentative and have difficulty getting along with one another in the confined and overcrowded environment. Every day the situation got worse. There was constant bickering, fighting, and noise. The noise alone was driving me crazy.

I had stopped two females from arguing and had exited their tank. As I closed the door, I noticed a female had slid a note under the door to me. As I read it, I thought, what now? The note stated that two females had threatened to push this female off the upstairs railing. The two females she accused had never given me any problems and I found this hard to believe, but I knew I had to go back into the tank to check it out. I entered the tank and started up the stairs. The noise was echoing off the walls.

I told the females to be quiet, but the noise continued. When I asked the two females about the threat, they denied it. I then walked over to the cell of the female who had stated she had been threatened. I tried to talk to her but there was so much noise I could not hear her. I stepped out of her cell and told the females again to be quiet, but the noise continued. Finally, I lost it.

I screamed as loud as I could and said, "Shut the hell up or I will lock everyone in their cells!" They looked at me as though I had lost my mind. I paused and then slowly walked down the stairs and out the tank door.

As soon as I had closed the tank door, I began to cry. I didn't want anyone to see me so I walked down the hallway and around the corner. I could not stop crying. In fact, I could not function. All I could think was that I had to get out of this place and I had to do it now! I was shaking like I was freezing and I could hardly breathe.

I knew I could not leave without notifying my sergeant so he could get someone to cover my area.

Finally, one of the male officers saw me. He and I had started to work at the jail on the same day and he was shocked to find me in this condition. He told me he would get the sergeant and asked me to wait there.

I was so embarrassed. I had always been able to keep my composure, but not this time. I wondered how I could get out of there without anyone seeing me.

The officer returned and escorted me to the sergeant's office. I entered his office feeling totally naked. He asked me what was wrong. I was still crying, but I managed to tell him I could not do this anymore.

He said, "Sure you can, you have been doing it all this time, haven't you?" He asked if I was having personal problems. I told him my personal life was not the issue. I just couldn't deal with the female inmates any longer. I asked him to let me go home.

He told me he would take care of the females. He called a couple of the male officers and they entered the female tank. My sergeant pulled the television out of the tank and locked all the females down. He then told me to go into my pod and write a report on the incident.

I entered my pod and walked up the three steps to my desk and sat down. From my desk, I could see the females peeking through their tiny windows. I felt bad because some of the females had not done anything wrong and yet they were all being punished.

I took a pen in my hand and tried to write, but I couldn't. I got up from my desk and walked down the three steps to my pod door and then turned around and walked back up the steps and sat down at my desk. Again, I got up from my desk and walked down the three steps. Then, I walked back up the steps. I looked out into the tank and realized several of the females were watching me.

I decided that it was time for me to go. If I was having a nervous breakdown, I did not want an audience.

As I walked down the hallway toward the elevator, another officer offered to escort me out of the building. I told him to tell the sergeant I may not ever return.

I cried all the way home and on into the night. I really didn't know why I was crying except I was so disappointed in myself.

The next day a friend came by to see me and I almost didn't open the door. When she entered the room, she asked, "Can I turn on the lights?"

I replied, "Sure, I didn't realize that they were off." We talked for a while and then she left.

The next two days were my regular days off. By the end of the second day, I began to think maybe I could return to work, but after the way I left, I wasn't sure I still had a job.

The next day, I put on my uniform and went to work. When I entered the jail, I felt that everyone was looking at me. Gossip in a jail spreads like wild fire.

When I reported for duty, I was summoned to the captain's office. As I entered her office, I noticed my sergeant had already arrived. She asked me to explain to her exactly what had happened the day I left. I told her I had been working the female area for three weeks straight, and I was frustrated and burned out.

She asked my sergeant why I had not been rotated. He said he did not realize I had not been rotated to a different area. I was encouraged to continue working at the jail and my sergeant was told to rotate all officers.

From that day on, I changed. I never allowed a situation to get out of control again. The females noticed I had changed and soon they began to change also. They knew I would take their television, write a disciplinary, or lock them down if that was what it took to keep the peace.

Later, I learned one of the females had started a rumor that they had locked me in a cell and I freaked out and went home. About a year later, the same female who had started the rumor returned to the jail. She apologized for telling the lie that started the rumor.

I'm proud to say I worked another seven and one-half years and never had another anxiety attack.

15

In a jail facility the stress level is very high. The inmates are the cause of a lot of the stress, but working with never enough officers to cover all areas causes unnecessary stress.

Most jails have this problem. Someone is always calling in sick, quitting their job, or getting fired for one reason or another. Then the officers on duty have to work two areas instead of one. Twice as many inmates, twice as much responsibility, and ten times the anger and stress.

Many arguments between officers and inmates or between two officers stemmed from not having enough officers on the shift. The security situation is unstable when there are not enough officers. This causes more stress.

It is very hard for an officer to control himself or herself and their anger when an inmate is up in their face calling them filthy names and refusing to follow any of the rules of the jail.

I always felt sorry for the new officers because learning a new job is stressful enough, but learning a new job while inmates are either making fun of you or harassing you while you work is almost impossible, but somehow, most got through it.

There were days I would get so angry with an inmate I would shake. Sometimes, I felt my hair was standing up on the top of my head. Sometimes I would play out a scenario in my mind that would relieve a little of my stress and anger toward an inmate or a situation that had occurred.

Each tank had a food pass on their door. The food pass was for passing the food trays, medications, requests, or talking to the inmate. It was approximately five inches wide and maybe fifteen inches long.

Many times, I have had arguments with an inmate through the food pass. He or she may have screamed in my face, kicked the door while I was talking with them through the food pass, or called me a "Mother Fucking Bitch." Any number of scenarios occurred over the course of my eight years at the jail.

Sometimes, I imagined a scenario in my mind that helped relieve some of the anger and stress. I called it "The Food Pass Fantasy."

In my mind, I would imagine I was pulling the head of an inmate who had given me hell all day long through the food pass. The inmate's head was larger than the food pass; therefore, I would have to pull very hard while his or her head was being squeezed. I imagined pulling on their head until it popped through to the other side. At that point, I would begin to feel a little relief.

When I was having problems with the whole tank, I would imagine I had one of those bean bag guns. All the inmates in the tank would be standing in line while I took aim. They would all be very afraid because they did not know I was using a bean bag gun. In no time at all, I had the whole tank under control in my mind, and I began to feel much better.

I shared my fantasy with one of the other officers who was having a really stressful day. She laughed at the thought of it, but I don't know if she ever used it. Maybe she made up her own fantasy. Hopefully it worked as well for her as mine did for me.

16

In a jail facility, contraband is always a problem. The inmates are constantly trying to get something they are not supposed to have.

We had one inmate who complained that he had problems with his feet and the shoes that were furnished by the jail did not give him enough support. The nurse finally agreed to allow him a pair of tennis shoes. His girlfriend dropped them off and I was called downstairs to pick them up and deliver them to the nurse.

It was the policy of the jail that anything brought into the jail should be inspected before giving it to an inmate. As I inspected the shoes, the nurse mentioned that I should check the soles. Upon inspection, I noticed the sole in one of the shoes was loose. I thought this was odd considering these were new shoes. As I pulled on the sole, I saw something that looked like plastic toward the toe of the shoe. With the help of the nurse, I pulled a plastic bag from under the sole of the shoe that contained marijuana. We immediately took the bag to the Jail Administrator and reported the incident. Charges were filed on the inmate's girlfriend and she was later arrested; the inmate continued to wear his county issued shoes.

* * *

When an inmate becomes a trustee and works out on the floor, rules require that he or she be patted down before returning them to their cell.

One day while patting down a male kitchen trustee, I felt something in his socks so I asked him to remove them. As he did so, out fell several pieces of lunchmeat and cheese. I asked if he had anything else hidden in his clothing or his body and told him if he would give it to me voluntarily, I would not write a disciplinary, but if it happened again he would no longer be a trustee. To my surprise, he pulled four pieces of bread out of his boxers. He told me he was hungry and begged me not to tell anyone. I let it ride that time, thinking anyone who would eat food pulled from the crotch of his underwear deserved one break.

* * *

Every day in the jail was not a bad day. Sometimes things happened that were quite comical.

Early one day an older female was booked in, but was being held in Solitary Confinement downstairs. For some reason, she was continuously flushing her toilet that caused the water to overflow and run out of her cell and into the hallway. The book-in officer saw the flooded hallway and called for the sergeant. I was standing with the sergeant when she received the call and she asked me to go with her to confront the situation.

As we entered her cell, we saw the inmate standing with one foot in the toilet as she continued to flush. A young male officer was trying to reason with her; the sergeant told her to stop flushing the toilet, yet she continued. I asked her to take her foot out of the toilet, but she refused. She told us that there was a line drawn on the floor and we had better not cross it. I looked down at the floor and saw no line. Either the line was imaginary or all the water had washed it away.

I stepped a little closer and she yelled, "Stop!" She glared at my sergeant and said, "Do you know Jesus?"

My sergeant answered, "Yes I do."

She then pulled up her blouse and yelled, "Well, here I am!" There she stood, braless, one foot still in the toilet. I heard someone laughing and it took me a moment to realize that it was me. I glanced over at the young male officer. His face was glowing from embarrassment as he walked away. I regained my composure as we restrained the female who was then moved to another area until she was bonded out.

※ ※ ※

Certain inmates, for various reasons, are kept in Solitary Confinement cells on the main floor. One male inmate was segregated because of psychological problems.

On one occasion, he called my name and motioned for me to come to his cell. When I looked through his cell window he was standing there totally naked with a strange look on his face. In his hands was his lunch tray and, proudly displayed on top of his mashed potatoes, was his penis. He appeared to be offering it to me as though he was a waiter serving hors d'oeuvres.

I merely looked at him and said politely, "No thank you," and walked away.

Another day, I was assigned to the sick tank, which contains inmates who are sick and also some who are mentally challenged. I was having a really stressful day because I was assigned to two areas. I was writing in my observation log when a motion caught my eye. I looked up and there were two of the mentally challenged inmates with sheets over their heads. They had torn holes in the sheets for their eyes and they were bobbing up and down in front of my window, laughing hysterically. I looked to my right and there was another inmate rotating from one foot to the other, swaying his hips in a circular motion, his body language saying "Everybody keep away."

The two in costume began gyrating and imitating his spastic routine. Soon the whole tank joined in and I was forced to disassemble this crazy dance group before it got out of hand.

I remember saying to myself, "If I don't lose my mind today, it will be because I lost it the day I took this job."

* * *

One afternoon, I was assigned to the Central Control area. The officer working this area is responsible for opening all the sliders, pod doors, and running the elevator.

He or she is also responsible for keeping male and female inmates separated by clearing the floor of male inmates when a female is on the floor. That day there were two male inmates on the floor as a female inmate came down the hallway. I told the male inmates to clear the floor. When I looked over at the men, one of them was standing there with a cardboard box over his head. Evidently he thought because his head was covered, he had become invisible. There were days when becoming invisible might have been a blessing.

***

A jail isn't a place where people normally burst into song, but occasionally it happens.

There was a freight elevator in the jail that went down to the kitchen. One day I took the elevator to the kitchen and as I exited, there were two male trustees standing at the elevator door. When they saw me, they began to sing, "If I were a carpenter and you were a lady, would you marry me anyway, would you have my baby?" One of them even got down on his knee as if he was really proposing. I tried not to encourage them, but I have to admit, they really did make my day. It's not every day that someone sings to you at work, especially in a jail.

***

One other time while I was working the sick tank, two inmates began to sing a rap song to me. At first, I tried to act like I hadn't noticed. Every so often, they would use my name in their song while swaying back and forth. I have to admit, I was impressed.

***

There was one inmate who was continually arrested for theft. I once watched the police chase him down in a department store parking lot. He was an older man and I don't know how he ran as fast as he did but he ran like a sprinter.

I asked him one time if he had ever considered doing something else for a living.

He looked at me, smiled and said, "What do you mean?"

"Well," I said, "you are obviously not good at what you are doing. If you were you would not constantly get caught." He turned to walk away. "Another thing," I said, "you are getting too old for this crap." He stopped and looked at me as though he was thinking about what I said.

Later that day, he was in the process of bonding out when I entered the book-in area. I told him not to come back. He turned and walked away. He was arrested again about nine months later.

* * *

There was an inmate in the sick tank who was mentally challenged. He called me over to the tank door to look at his drawings. (Many of the inmates have artistic talent; some drew beautiful, ornate designs on their envelopes to their loved ones, though none compared with his.) The people he drew appeared to be similar to paintings like the Mona Lisa by Da Vinci.

I encouraged him to enter drawing and painting contests when he was released.

I had the feeling he had never received any encouragement for his talent. He seemed out of place in this world, almost as though he belonged to another time, a time when life was simple and carefree.

* * *

There was a trustee at the jail everybody called "Chicken George." He could not read and could barely write his name. Whenever he received a letter, he had to get someone to read it. Quite often, he would ask me if I had the time to read his letter to him. I would take the time because I knew how much those letters meant to him. He could have asked another officer or an inmate to read the letters, but perhaps he didn't want them to know his business.

I would read them like I was reading a story from a book. I would put more emphasis on certain words and that would make him laugh. We both enjoyed those letters.

* * *

There was one inmate who visited our jail quite often. He would do his time—get out of jail—and within two or three months, he would be back. He walked up to me one day and said, "I never do nothin' wrong, I don't know why they keep arrestin' me." I had to laugh because he was so serious about it. I acted like I could not understand why they kept arresting him either.

I said, "Maybe you're just unlucky."

"My whole family must be unlucky," he answered. "Both my brothers been in prison for somethin' they didn't do, neither. I hear you can get a good education in prison."

"That may be true, but wouldn't it be easier to do that in the real world?"

"Too many distractions in the real world," he replied.

So many of the repeat offenders lack a decent education and have no one to encourage them to better themselves.

* * *

You tend to see a lot of strange people in jails.

One of the young male officers working the Maximum Security area told me he was walking through one of the tanks while getting his head count when an inmate ejaculated through his food pass toward him.

I asked the officer, "What did you do?"

He said, "I jumped back and said you missed me you Son of a Bitch." We both laughed.

* * *

As I exited the elevator to the book-in area one day, I saw a man standing there with long tacky hair, makeup all over his face, and totally naked. Well, he wasn't totally naked. He had something that looked like a fig leaf covering his private area. The book-in officer told me he also had a purse with him that had a dildo in it.

I could just imagine how silly the officer that brought him in must have felt escorting a naked man carrying a purse.

* * *

When someone is arrested, all of their personal property is taken from them.

Contraband is a real problem in jails and prisons.

One female in particular managed to hide her lipstick from the book-in officer and then bring it up with her to her cell. She had visited our jail many times and each time she managed to make it through booking with her lipstick.

I noticed her lips were always red and she would try to convince me that she used Vaseline and map colors to color her lips, but I knew better.

After a while, I would wait for her to be booked in and then I would go to her cell and ask for the lipstick, although I had not yet seen any evidence that she had it with her. I would tell her that I knew that she had it and that I would not write a disciplinary if she would give it to me. She didn't argue about it, she just handed it over. I asked her how she managed to hide it from the book-in officer every time. She stated that she hid it in her vagina.

* * *

Fruit is served with many of the inmate meals. Some of the inmates would hide their fruit until it fermented and then make bootleg wine. A quick cell search did not always result in finding the contraband.

The officer would notice that the inmates were in an unusually pleasant mood, which offered the officer a reprieve from the daily confusion.

17

When an inmate leaves the jail to go to the doctor or the hospital, a transport officer, or sometimes a detention officer, has to stay with the inmate no matter what procedure they are having. A female officer may have to spend her working day in a hospital room with a male inmate.

I was assigned to sit with an inmate all day in the hospital who had a colostomy done the day before because of cancer. I was a little uncomfortable about spending all day in his room knowing I would not be able to smoke and would probably go through withdrawal before the day was over. I decided to try to make the best of it because I really had no choice.

At one time, this inmate had been our floor trustee, so we were not strangers. He seemed to be in a pretty good mood considering all that he had gone through, but he could sense I was a little uncomfortable.

He called me to the side of his bed and showed me what appeared to be an intestine hanging out the side of his lower stomach. Had I been a nurse this sight may not have affected me, but as I was not a nurse, the sight really upset me.

After a while, the nurse arrived and began to explain to the inmate the manner in which he had to connect the colostomy bag. I was looking at the inmate while she spoke with him. All of a sudden, he began to have a bowel movement out of the intestine that was hanging out of the side of his stomach. It was in liquid form and was spurting all over him.

I felt a sudden urge to run out of the room, but I knew that I couldn't so I just sat there. The odor consumed the room and, at one point, I gagged. The inmate was embarrassed and so was I. It didn't seem to bother the nurse. It happened again two more times before the day was over. Each time there would be a bubbling noise and then once again the room was consumed with the foul odor. I had to go into the bathroom and gag every so often. Between the gagging and the nicotine withdrawal, it was a very, very long day.

* * *

Another incident that stands out in my mind was when I transported a female to the doctor's office. Shortly before being arrested in another state, she had a breast implant operation and by the time she was delivered to us, she had developed a very bad infection in her right breast.

I had to stay in the room with her while the doctor examined her. He removed a bandage that was covering an incision that had been made in her breast. Without being given a sedative, he mashed on her breast with his hand and a yellowish mucus substance oozed out. He then stuck his fingers inside the incision and pulled strands of gauze out of her breast. At that point, I began to feel nauseated and a little dizzy.

After he removed all the gauze, he stuck his hand inside her breast and raked out more yellowish substance. I could see his knuckles moving beneath the skin. She lay there, not making a sound. I could see the pain etched across her face. I thought I might pass out myself, I was feeling very weak in the knees. The nurse gave me a chair and told me to sit down. I sat there facing the wall for the rest of the procedure.

I had once considered breast implants myself, but after witnessing what this woman went through, I realized that it was definitely not worth the risk.

18

Several officers from our jail were sent out of town to take a Defensive Tactics Course along with officers from surrounding cities. Myself and one other female were the only two women taking the course. The class was very similar to the training given to peace officers. We learned the names and locations of all the pressure points on the body and how to use them. We also learned how to defend ourselves in case we were attacked.

The instructor would call me to the front of the class and practice using the pressure points on my body. I honestly felt that he enjoyed inflicting pain on others.

He stated that he had worked undercover for years before becoming an instructor. He showed us a scar that ran four inches across his neck, which had almost caused his death. While he was working undercover, a drug dealer had come from behind and slit his throat.

On our last day, we were all told to gather in a circle. There were several mats lying on the floor. He was wearing a protective suit and helmet. We were wearing only a protective helmet. We were told that one of us at a time would have to defend ourselves against him. Because he was so intimidating I was dreading the confrontation.

I watched as one officer at a time entered the middle of the circle. He would give them a scenario to follow. For instance: You are trying to lock down the tank, but there is one inmate who will not go into his or her cell. What do you do? At that point, the officer was supposed to use the Defensive Tactics that had been taught. Basically, most of the scenarios were similar and the tactics used in these situations were mainly the usage of pressure points.

I was beginning to feel a little better about the whole situation. I remember thinking, "I can do this."

He called my name and I entered the center of the circle. Before I knew what was happening, he was in my space. His face was about one inch from mine. In a very sadistic, gruff voice, he said, "I am going to rip all of your clothes off and I am going to screw you like you have never been screwed before and you are going to like it."

I was shocked and dumbfounded. I just stood there like an idiot. I could not understand why he had spoken to me in that manner. He had not spoken that way to any of the other officers, including the other female officer.

Before I had time to get my senses together, he hit me in the head twice with his fist. The protective helmet absorbed some of the shock, but not all of it. Again, I just stood there.

I could hear him saying, "Aren't you going to do something? Is this what I taught you?"

As I glanced around, I realized that all the other officers were looking at me. I was totally humiliated. Finally, I said, "No, this is not what you taught me."

He said, "Turn around and face the wall. I am going to attack you from behind, but you will not know when."

I stood there facing the wall for what seemed like a long time. He was stalking back and forth while mumbling something that I could not understand. At times, I could feel him breathing on my neck. "I have to be ready for him this time," I thought. I was shaking all over, but not just out of fear. My anger had turned into rage. At that moment, I actually hated this man.

All of a sudden, he grabbed me! I jabbed him in the ribs with my elbow and then turned around and kicked him. I don't really remember what happened after that. We were at one end of the mat and the next thing I knew, we were at the other end. I was on top of him, beating him with my fists.

I had passed the test. The protective suit he was wearing had kept him from being injured, so he was just fine. I was an emotional wreck, but he was just fine.

Now I had to take the written part of the test. I was afraid that I would not be able to concentrate considering I was still upset from the fight we just had. I really believe that he planned it that way. Somehow, I managed to pass the written part of the course.

Thank God, this whole ordeal was over.

He tried to act friendly toward me as we left, but I really had no use for him. He mentioned that he would be happy to come down to the jail next year for the Defensive Tactics Course. I told him I would mention it to the Jail Administrator, but I never did.

This class lasted for three days at the end of which I was so sore I could barely move. In fact, on the second day after I got home I cried. I had arthritis in my joints, which caused inflammation, and it was increasingly getting worse.

I remembered a question that I had read in a book at one time. The question was, "If you could say Goodbye, goodbye, and a person that you really disliked would disappear and you would not be punished, would you do it? My answer concerning this man is "Goodbye, goodbye."

19

Female officers are assigned to both male and female areas. There were several incidents with the female inmates that were, if not really frightening, at least odd.

I have known some female inmates that had split personalities. One time they would seem normal and suddenly, another personality would emerge that appeared to be a little girl.

One female in particular would be talking to me about some problem that concerned her and then she would seem to forget what she was going to say, pause for a moment and then continue the conversation as a little girl who was afraid to speak her mind.

At first, I didn't understand. But, after being around her for a while, I learned that she wasn't aware that this was happening. When she acted as a little girl, I spoke to her as if I were speaking to a child. This seemed to comfort her.

Another female also had an alternate child personality. She thought everyone was mistreating her; therefore, she cried much of the time. Each night I would walk through the tank and lock all the females in their cells. As I closed their doors, most of them would say good night. I would repeat good night back to them.

As I passed another cell, I heard a little voice say, "Good night, I love you." I said good night, but ignored the "I love you" because as an officer, I really had to remain detached.

The next night I was walking through the tank again locking all the females down when I heard the little girl voice at her cell door. Again, she said, "Good night, I love you." I looked at her face and noticed she was crying.

I heard that several of the females would be transported to the prison and her name was on the list. We were not allowed to tell the inmates when they would be leaving and I realized this was going to be very hard for her. The night before she was to be transferred we went through the same routine, only this time I answered, "Good night, I love you, too." She smiled her little girl smile. When I checked on her later that night, she was sleeping soundly.

About a year later, I was working the visitation area when a woman walked up to me. I assumed that she was there to visit someone. At first, I didn't recognize her, but then I remembered the little girl personality. She said, "I just wanted you to know that I am okay, and I want to thank you for being so good to me." I told her that it was good to see her. She hugged me and then walked away. I never saw her again.

* * *

One day I was called to the elevator to escort a female to her cell. As we walked down the hallway toward the female tank, I asked her if she was okay. She looked down at the floor and began to cry uncontrollably. She told me that she had returned from court and had received a sentence of ten years.

I tried to console her. She grabbed me and hugged me as though I was her mother. She cried, "I won't make it, I won't make it. I can't do ten years."

She was a young woman, only twenty-one years old, and now her life would never be the same again. Hugging a prisoner is against all the rules, but sometimes you just have to be a human being.

* * *

There was another female who had visited our facility many times. On her last visit, there were rumors that she was bi-sexual. One day, she handed me a note and asked me to read it before I left for the day. When I read it, I was a bit shocked.

The note stated that she thought that I was a very nice person and appreciated my kindness toward her. She asked if she could write me on a personal level. She also said that no one would ever have to know about it. Toward the end of the note, she declared that she loved me.

I don't know why I had not seen this coming. There were times that she did seem to go out of her way to talk to me. At first, I couldn't decide what to do about the situation, but finally decided to take the note to my sergeant. She told me to return the note to the inmate.

I called her out into the hallway, away from the other females, and spoke with her. Although I was not interested, I did not want to hurt her feelings. I told her that we could never have that kind of relationship and that I could not accept the note. She appeared to be a little embarrassed, but I thought she understood. I realized later that she held a grudge against me. She had a bad attitude from that day on, and was argumentative and disruptive any time I encountered her.

20

Locking the inmates down for the night is not always a pleasant experience. Like children, they do not want anyone telling them that it is time to go to bed. The male inmates know that if a female officer is working their area, she will be the officer walking through to make sure they are in their cells before lockdown. Many times, as I walked through, a male inmate would make sure he had his erect penis exposed while standing over the urinal. This was his way of exposing himself and getting away with it. He could always use the excuse that he had to use the bathroom and could not wait.

There was one thing I noticed while locking down that really surprised me. As I passed by the cells, some of the male inmates would be down on their knees praying before they went to sleep and this was in the Maximum Security area. They would raise hell all day long and yet humble themselves before God each night.

I have seen so many inmates become religious while they are in jail. They tend to live a righteous life and even witness to other inmates while they are incarcerated.

They read the Bible daily and try to avoid conflict with other inmates but as soon as they are released back into society, it is all forgotten, and most fall back into their old lifestyles. A few inmates carry their religion with them when they leave the jail, though not many.

Sometimes when I saw an inmate return to jail, I felt sad, because, for some, this is the essence of the rest of their lives. What a waste!

21

When I first started working in the jail, I thought I could get through to some of the inmates and possibly make a difference in their lives. If I saw inmates doing something wrong, I would stop them. They did not always appreciate it, but most of them realized I was only doing my job.

I finally realized one thing I could do was to set an example. The officers had standard operating procedures (SOP), just as the inmates had their rules to follow.

Some of the officers would bend the rules daily, which really upset me. How could an officer expect the inmates to follow the rules of the jail if he or she doesn't follow them?

Some of the officers felt sorry for the inmates and looked the other way when an inmate was doing something wrong. Others ignored the situation because they did not want to take the time to write a disciplinary report.

I felt the officers encouraged the inmates to do wrong by looking the other way. Most of the inmates were very accomplished in doing the wrong thing. Somebody has to set the right example; it is one of the responsibilities of a detention officer, but not everybody accepted that responsibility.

I have seen so many types of officers working in the jail. Some of them appear to be on a power trip. They really enjoy bossing the inmates. These officers can stir up a lot of trouble but they don't usually last too long as officers. For one reason or another, they tend to get into some kind of trouble and eventually lose their jobs.

There are other officers who become too close to the inmates and gradually become more like an inmate than an officer. Some of these officers eventually commit crimes themselves.

Then there are the good officers who take their job seriously and try to do the best they can. Life is harder for these officers because if they are doing everything the way it is supposed to be done, when they attempt to control a situation which was ignored by a previous officer, it appears to the inmates that they are being picked on. They become argumentative or aggressive, causing stress for the officer.

The inmates also play one officer against the other. Sometimes it seems that there is a popularity contest going on between the officers. The inmates convince one officer that another officer is trashing him behind his back, stating that he can't handle his job. This is a real insult to the officer because handling situations is the biggest part of the job description. This causes conflict. The inmates are easily bored and if they can cause an argument, they have produced and directed their own entertainment.

22

When I think back on my eight years at the county jail, I realize that I have changed in many ways. I have hardened, but I have learned so much.

First, we all make mistakes. There are times people use bad judgment and have to suffer the consequences. Although not always aware of the individual crimes, I have learned not to judge others by their mistakes. Second, at times good people do bad things and sometimes, bad people do terrible things. I still believe that most people have some good in them. Most important, I really don't see different races anymore, I just see people. I don't know how other officers are affected by their experiences in the jail. I can only speak for myself.

After several years of working at the jail, I had built walls as boundaries to protect myself. It was easier for me to handle my job if I didn't allow myself to feel any attachment toward the inmates.

During that time I would pass a cell knowing an inmate was locked down separated from the other inmates, and had been for several days, and would not feel any compassion. There was nothing I could do about it. I would tell myself he or she probably deserved it.

I began to realize I had changed. I no longer felt good about the person I had become. This had also become evident in my personal life. I was short-tempered, intolerant, and found myself treating my family like they were unruly inmates. I made the decision to quit the job to salvage myself.

Little by little, I began to allow myself to feel again. I am now a more caring and compassionate person than I was before I went to work at the jail.

In a way I feel I did eight years hard time. There were days and nights that were so bad I didn't think I would survive. I also felt I was locked in with no windows to view the outside world. Yet, there were also other times I felt needed and had hope that I was making a difference.

There are so many of the inmates that I will never forget, some because they were so downright mean, and others who could not find their direction in life. I will also remember all the officers who put their heart and soul into their work. They continue to work very hard and receive very little recognition.

In some ways, it was like going to war together; some were casualties and others managed to survive. After leaving, you may occasionally speak about your war wounds among your fellow survivors, but basically you try to get on with your life and act as though it never happened.

Printed in the United States
56292LVS00010B/154-162